Bachelard Interpreted 6

The Kiss Reverberant

Frank Prem

Wild Arancini Press
2025

Publication Details

Title: The Kiss Reverberant: Bachelard Interpreted Book 6
ISBN: 978-1-923166-26-4 (p-bk)
ISBN: 978-1-925963-73-1 (e-bk)

Published by Wild Arancini Press
Copyright © 2025 Frank Prem
All rights reserved:

No part of this publication may be reproduced, stored in a retrieval system, or transmitted in any form or by any means, electronic, mechanical, photocopying, recording or otherwise, without prior written permission from the publisher and author.
A catalogue record for this book is available from the National Library of Australia.

Cover Concept: Wild Arancini Press
Cover Image AI assistant: Adobe Firefly

It has always been about time.

CONTENTS

The Kiss Reverberant

Introduction 1

Intuition of the Instant

what time when 5
'instant' pillars 6
reality now 7
that is all 8
now and then 10
celling a memory 11
is gone 12
recurrence 13
instant back 14
in the moment 16
endured instantly 17
with the help of the teacher 18
alive now 19
the time traveller reflects 20
a moment of memory 22
yesterday? 23
only now 24
if because 25
just a moment 26
neverendsitgoeson 27
last points 29
four eyes on the moment 30
now, is 32
is was 33

the way to creativity.. 34
the kiss reverberant... 36
the seed's perception.. 37
being (shakespeare) 38
refuting a shallow instant..................................... 39
being in instants 40
dogmatic slumbers 41
zones 42
in support.. 44
what I know 45
versus the construct... 46
uncompressed and all included 47
gravity dance... 49
one-plus-ones 50
substantive... 51
perspective (I see time).. 52
remember was... 53
pinpointed.. 54
the chore rebuilt 55
in an instant.. 56
finding myself backwards..................................... 57
consequent 59
nothing (at all)... 60
the novel one.. 61
an event 63
see nothing 64
your moment waits 65
nothing (happening now)..................................... 67
an hour of something.. 68
tick tock... 69
specimen of time 70

the white space	72
two things (synchronicity)	73
a wall against	75
counting	76
on a continuum	78
synchronicitous	79
what was, is	80
multiply/divide	82
maybe me (in another moment)	84
worrying times	85
my illusion, I believe	86
music of the duration	87
to be (for just a moment)	88
aware of	89
now now	90
reading now	91
when am I	92
old note:new chord	93
surely swirly	94
at present	96
forever	97
the loss	98
same again	99
learned time	100
beyond a shape, the senses	101
right now	102
enduring	103
habit	104
just like	105
etching a return	107
being and becoming	109

seed	110
to achieve the silence (of a violin)	111
thirst the disintegration	112
learning to walk (creating a follower)	113
wait … 'then'	114
instant belief	115
tattoo life	116
newborn breeze	117
enscribed	118
habitually me	119
juiced up (as I recall)	120
memory of being	121
accidentally me	122
predictable change	123
the habit of remembering	125
none like now	126
accidentally here	127
fleet	128
a habit of being (here)	129
accidentally	130
together for a moment	131
me (approximately)	132
a trace of me	133
better	134
aware the moment	135
each I know	136
as change	137
woven	138
duration, habit and progress	139
you I know	141
is mystery	142

mine now 143

The Dialectic of Duration

pushing for change 147
one moment - an intuition (of autumn) 149
wishing (the end) away 151
wandering 153
instant nothing 155
years ago 156
the problem (with his hat) 158
un-stopped: the rightness 160
temporary permanent destruction 162
endurance found 164
more is less 166
was (gone) 167

Bachelard Source Materials 169

Author Information 171

Other Published Works 173

What Readers Say 175

The Kiss Reverberant

Introduction

French scientist and philosopher Gaston Bachelard (1884 - 1962) explored and examined poetics and poetry in great depth over the course of his lifetime, particularly examining the poetics of natural elements, of which he identified the four that are traditionally considered:

Fire
Water
Air, and
Earth.

In addition, however, he (effectively) identified two further elements, or dimensions, for his examinations:

Time, and
Space

The *Bachelard Interpreted* poetry series responds to each of these elements and dimensions, and also encompasses certain other writings undertaken by Bachelard, encompassing some of his further scientific and literary undertakings.

The Kiss Reverberant explores aspects of time. Not strictly examining the poetics of time, but nonetheless inspiring contemplation of the myriad meanings of a moment, an instant, and the different forms that the effects of time might have on a lived poetic experience.

The poetry in this collection explores transformation through reverie. The imagery released is, at times, astonishing.

Note: *The Kiss Reverberant* is one of a series of poetry collections inspired by the work of Gaston Bachelard. References to the Bachelard translations that have been relied on as source materials for this project are listed at the end of this book.

Intuition of the Instant

what time when

yester-nothing

tomorrow-nothing

now

the void
has swallowed
everything
that ever was

the void
is holding
everything
to come

me?

> *I am only now*
> *I am only now*
> *I am only now*

once I was
then
which is gone

once
I will be
that

sometime

sometime
this time
was
just now

'instant' pillars

it is a pillar

they are
all pillars

they are relentless . . .

marching
at me
all the time

absorbing me

me
alone in solitude

leaving *me*
a memory
of a distorted pillar
of one moment
back
in time

pillar pillar pillar
marching moments

take me in

hold me

throw me out

march on
march on
march time

reality now

it was a game of sorts

reality lay hidden
behind a pillar
of past fragments

      step   *step*   *step*

keeping up
but staying
out of the sight
of
now

now
was an un-real moment

a displacement
always

      step   *step*   *step*

becoming itself
differently
again

unreal
unreal

but [GRAB]
time has a way
in every passing instant
of reaching
and touching

making an odd
displacement
now-real

that is all

can it be

    deader than death

perhaps . . .

if it has never *been*

I know it well —
I *lived* it —
but . . .

it is gone
and what remains
is only
now

inside *my* head
and mine alone

I am the only one
who saw it
and even *I*
can't know
what it is
that I *recall*

the *real* of it
is gone —
it never *was* —
and memory
has a palette
to paint anything
that it wants

it is deader than dead
I know
now
that it never occurred

The Kiss Reverberant

mirage
illusion
fantasy

that is all

deader than dead
and *that*
is all

now and then

a moment comes

and then . . .

it goes

it wasn't *here*
it just
became

it is gone

mourned
by a hollow wind
that blows
joyless echoes
of neither
the moment
nor
a true recall

it is gone

and the life that lived
within
is . . .

no more

no more
than a hollow reverberation
blown mournfully
away

as dust
into the barren landscape
so intimately known
as *then*

celling a memory

in his mind
he drew an image

then another
almost identical

he drew another . . .

again

cell after cell
all *nearly* the same

slight differences
of instant
following instant

when he had drawn
assembled
scanned
each image
he was *capable*

was *able*
to recall –
complete –
the memory of a thing
that happened once

meanwhile

time
had passed

is gone

now
is gone
now
is gone
now
is gone

now

looking back
it all happened
so
quickly

everything
became different
all the time

nothing
stayed the same
and even
now

recurrence

time stands

I know I have
already
done this

again

this
has all
happened

just so

before

here it comes
it comes

the *recurrence*
and
I know it

time stands and I
am doing it
again

instant back

if I could have
one instant
back

one instant
to hold
to me

if I could ratchet
the hand of time
one tick

maybe I would change
my mind
that fateful day

maybe I would choose
to hold that instant close

to be there
again
when I blink my eyes
be there again
when I blink
my eyes
be there again . . .

or
would it be best
to let it go

am I better
to hold an *idea* –
instead –
of that moment

what am I to do
with a pocketful
of old instants

The Kiss Reverberant

would I *really* do well
to go back there

to *do*
back there
again

if I could have
one instant back
I hope . . .

I hope . . .

I hope that I would
let it
go

just
let it go

in the moment

what lives
in an instant of time?

is it a mite
or a moment?
a life
or a breath
of the wind passing by?

in a bit –
just a second –
the immediate
this instant I say

    right now

what life
has just happened?

what life
is but an idea
away?

in an instant
the whole of revelation

the *all*
of what *was* nothing
now a something
that passed by
just *then*

a life
lived in an instant –
a moment
a second
just now –

is just me

endured instantly

is a collection of instants
a life?

a single-file regiment
marching
through time

the whole
so much more
than its parts

what is *now*
but the hesitation
that happens
between *what has been*
and
what is to come?

a nothing
that separates
every everything

is a life
all of its instants
endured?

with the help of the teacher

at what point
in my life
did I know
that?

once upon a time –
I know –
I did not

once upon another time –
perhaps –
I wondered

and once upon . . .

well
now
I know I know

but
when did I pass
from the *first* state
to the *second*
into *me*
at this time?

time *does* nothing
time is the teacher

over time I
have come
to know

alive now

is it only
now
that I am
alive

what was I
yesterday?

one cell in a movie
played
backward and forward
and over and over
then rewound

degraded –
just a small amount –
with each replay

what will I be
tomorrow

a will-o-the-wisp

a phantom

almost solid
and almost real
but
changing –
a *chimera* –
with every glimpse

only *now*

only now
I
am alive

the time traveller reflects

travelling
back through time
is such a drag

don't you agree?

oh
it has its uses

that
I know

> *small corrections*
> *here and there*
>
> *smoother trails*
> *into the sunset*
> *that can't be changed*

yeah yeah

yeah

but
don't show *yourself*
to *younger you*

don't reveal your face
to anyone
you know

to anyone
you once knew

lest they double-take
and change
the big continuum
of space
and *then-and-there*
or *here-and-now*

The Kiss Reverberant

god help you
if you show —
just *once* —
who you are
to anyone at all
that might matter
in your life

maybe
in *their* life

and
how are you to know?

yaah

it's overrated
so
why don't you
and I
settle down somewhere
right now

and get to know
what *this* little moment
brings

to the full
and with no regrets
that might need
a tweaking
later

there's nothing
later

let's do it
now

a moment of memory

that moment
that was
nothing
abuts against
a moment
that was
nothing for an instant
touching
another moment
that equals *nothing*
at all

how long
can these *nothings* last?

will
a moment
plus a moment
plus a moment
make sixty seconds
or a minute?

how many does it take
to make
one hour
of this day?

how many
to make and keep
a memory . . .

one that endures beyond
a moment
that
is nothing?

yesterday?

do I know
that life existed
yesterday?

I remember clearly
that it did

the details
of the day I had

the time I spent
talking –
so earnestly –
with you

but *that* was then

but
was that
then

what I recall –
was that a real life
or some *thing*
my mind made up
to fill a space
that I name

> *the memory*
> *of yesterday?*

maybe that life

this life

was *never*
really
until I thought
today

only now

I feel now
I
feel alive

I thought
that thought was true
yesterday

but yesterday fades . . .

a ghost at play

there is no life
in memory

I feel
now
I feel
alive

I can touch
and know
what life is
with a fingertip

and I recall
everything I felt
just a day before

but
as much as that
was . . .

. . . *alive*
is now

I feel my life
I feel *only*
now

if because

if today *is*
because
yesterday *was*
then
who am I
at present?

> *the product*
> *of a line*
> *that has gone before?*
>
> *a new eye-opening*
> *to cast*
> *a fresh gaze*
> *across the world?*

maybe
maybe
but
right now I believe
in tomorrow
and

I am waiting

just a moment

of this
you can be clear
that moment
was
a moment

I saw it
in the distance

I saw it
as it came closer

I saw it
as I lived it

I can see it –
fading
out of sight –
as I shade my eyes
to look ahead
into the blazing sun

that moment

what a moment

I saw it

now
it's gone

neverendsitgoeson

*does time
only go forward?*

he wondered

*can it also go
backward
to the past?*

*are there dimensions
off to one side?*

surely *backward*
is only the past

and *forward*
is only
a predictable
tomorrow

what else
does
the passage of time?

does it eternally
pass
can it *linger*

a loop
a twirl
round a moment
particularly enjoyable

particularly provocative

particularly nothingeverendsitgoeson

just like a goldfish
moments repeated
as fresh as the time
they were born

again

again

perhaps
time only goes forward
for a reason

maybe it is to save
a man's mind
from the fire

the abyss

once
around the clock

that's the way

last points

how many points
can be plotted
on a line?

how long
can an instant
last?

where does the circle
finally end?

how could I appreciate
yesterday
while I was
still there?

I can see me *then*
shaded sepia

I can see *you*
in old-fashioned clothes

how much smiling
at the camera
will bring a picture
to life?

four eyes on the moment

come
stand here
right beside me

we will share
a moment

you will look
and I will look

together

at the *same* moment

later
we can review
what we saw

in 4d

quadro-scope

your view
will be nothing like
mine

so close
but
not *real*

too real

were you watching
my moment

I don't think so

The Kiss Reverberant

I
didn't see your moment
either
and I
didn't see my moment
either
I only glimpsed
a replay
of something

I'm sorry

I thought that we could
share
one moment

now, is

what if this life
is only *now*
in the moment
and as I think of it?

what if *you*
are only
because I see you
right now?

right now
is gone
in the instant
that I wrote it

there it is . . .

no it's gone again

what can I capture?

is there an adequate jar?
a sufficient
stopper?

is it any kind
of wonder
I grow tired
living only
in these never-ending instants
back-to-back
to-back-to-back . . .

it takes no time
no time at all
yet
there is no peace
from *being*
if this life
is *only*

is was

did *now* happen
only
because of *then?*

I think
I understand my *then*
through *now*

am I
I am
because the past

or
was I
I was
because I *now?*

I look back
at images

they cannot explain
the *who* I am
by showing
what I *was*

I
does not exist
that way

for I
am here
and now

the way to creativity

it builds and it builds
as I do
and I do

it grows
from conception
to fact

and though it starts
something small
it gathers
in strength

momentum
will drive

bullock through

but wait . . .

just wait

that is not right
no no no

each thing
is
its *own* thing

each thought is conceived
alone
there is no
one
plus one
equaling four

an idea by itself
is a spark
not a fire

The Kiss Reverberant

try another
then
add
just another
before you can see
what you've got

these ideas are
each
put together

they are one
but . . .

engineering
is not avalanche

I
come as a storm

>	*one*
>	*and one*
>
>	*I*
>	*will sweep you away*
>	*creatively*
>
>	*build*
>	*create and construct*

an idea

the kiss reverberant

intimate
infinite
the kindness of a blow
kissed
through a wielding
of the hammer

nothing is the same
beyond the moment

the ringing
of the anvil
is only an echo

the sound
of such a sweet kiss
a bell into the distance . . .

forever

changing every-*thing*
and every-*where*

changing in small ways
every-*when*
there ever is
or was

intimate

infinite

the kiss
that was a hammer blow
is a kindness
reverberant
through time

the seed's perception

my world is held
within an arc
of the sky

sometimes –
almost –
I do not see it
I do not feel it

but
the blue above –
I know –
is a curving dome
that loses the horizon

I cannot touch it
though I know
that it is there

I cannot strike it
with the stone I throw –
propelled with all the wrath
an arm can hurl –

one day
I'm going to break out

one day
I swear
that I'll be free
beyond the blue

beyond the arc

out there
I will encounter
no restrictions
no constraints
on me

being (shakespeare)

being . . .

not being

a state of mind
gone past
in just a moment

make a choice

> *be*
> *what you might be*

make a choice

> *be nothing*

time

passes in an instant
and you
might have been
that one

I
might be the next

you and I
might
let it pass us by
while we
are *being*

not being

refuting a shallow instant

nothing can happen
in an instant

it is too short
for time

too
instantaneous

and
it can have
no depth

wait . . .

what
just happened?

when?

how long
did that take?

no time
at all

being in instants

why do I
need time

that only comes
and goes?
that washes clean every instant
before it?

leaves no sign
of where it's been?

it's just *a new*
and *a new*
and *a new*
for *ever*

why do I need time?

when
am I to be more
than just
living?

I guess that
I am
only within
my time

I am a *be*-ing
only in my instants

dogmatic slumbers

I insist
that I am sleeping

I don't believe I am awake

this is the passage
of a dream I see go by
before me

there is no chance
that I'm mistaken

I am convinced I know
my self

if *you* are *here*
it is as a figment
of the mind

no no
don't try
to persuade me

no no I *know*
and *you* are wrong

no
asleep is what I am
until by-and-by

if you are still here
when I awaken
then I will listen
to what you say
but now
I must insist
that I don't believe
I am awake

begone

zones

he lived
in time zones

thousands
of time zones

every thought he thought
(like this one)
a time zone

not the same
as the time zone he utilised
for this thought

or
for that one

he wondered
in another

how loud must it be

>   *if each*
>   *made its own sound*
>   *zipping its way*
>   *to oblivion*

he wondered
if ever there could be
collision
at a crossroads
a roundabout

dead end

a convergence

he wondered
whatever happens to them

The Kiss Reverberant

to all the individual
time zones

and he wondered too
whatever happens
to hers

might they meet his
one day

oh
happy day

oh

happy day

in support

I am here
because
the air around me

I am here
because
the ground

here
I am

the time ticks
me
and so

air and time
and earth
within my heart
right now
right here
right this
I am
right that

do you feel the breeze
running through your fingers?

do you comprehend the place
you stand?

can you think of when
or
then and now
in a single breath?

are *you* here
because?

what I know

being
in the right here
this time
this place

only now
because then
I was
or
then perhaps
I will be

but
right now
I do not know

versus the construct

not here
tomorrow

not there
today

everywhere
all the time
so long as
now

nowhere
then

me
versus the construct
I know differently
every time

uncompressed and all included

she held in her hand
an instant
of time

held it gentle
firm

carefully

twirling spinning tugging
from both ends
she uncompressed

slow coaxing
long
wide

she put the stars inside . . .

the sun
and the moon

put love within

inserted tedium
as well

in she went
with the feelings that come
and go
like that

everything . . .

she inserted everything
that she knew
to fill
and overflow a day
and a night

then
she let that instant
go

let it start
whenever
it wished

gravity dance

as the stars
pirouette
the sun

so the sun
in circles
adores the earth

tied
on a line
like a ball
on a string

with the moon
in support role
through the night

dance
you stars
around the sun
where it shines
too bright
in the sky

dance you sun
caper
on the end
of the line

you will not dance free
no no
while gravity
holds the wire

one-plus-ones

an event
where nothing happened

a moment
that took no time
at all

what *are* these things?
what
do they mean?

is *duration*
filled with emptiness . . .

with the empty time
of *no time left*
at all?

how many one-plus-ones
does it take
to equal
something that happens?

how many moments
to make
a while?

how many
does it take
for me to contemplate?

I'll tell you
in the moment
that something happens

in the moment
that I know

substantive

to be *some-thing*
she had to *be*
something

for
how could she *be*
if she was *no*-thing?

how can *nothing* be?

and what was she?
and which was she?

perhaps
a place-mark
on the circle route
of a journey

passing through
and then return

searching the *out*-ward

scouring the *in*
for traces
of a substance
that was her
alone

perspective (I see time)

over time
I see
time

up close –
when it is happening –
I see nothing

there is only *me*
here

but
looking back I see
this and that
and you yourself

I watch you
afloat among
the things we did
and you are
there

I see you

I understand
just who you were
to *me*
through time

up close
there is only me
here
and a shadow
in my light
where you stand

so close
in time

remember was

I remember

I remember that I
was

like an echo
of being

but I do not know
how long
between that
then
and *now*

I remember
a moment when *I*
was

but I don't recall
the *time*
I was

perhaps I was
as long as
not at all

pinpointed

I dreamed a constellation
in my head

I arranged each pin
of brightness
just so

the horse
the wolf
the shape
that matched the outline
of my heart

with every beat
a new array arisen

and I dreamed
that I contained
all the things
they were

what need for me
to gaze up
to the sky at night
when I carry
all of the stars?

the chore rebuilt

every minute
he would forget

every second
he remembered

he would never
know
but would attempt
to reconstruct
the *who*
that he *was*
by the who
he had *been*
in different moments

a swirling chronology
of himself
built up again

and up
again

only staying
true
for the time it took
to build up again

and *new*
all the time

the building task
extended by the incessant
new

being

such a weariness

his chore

in an instant

she reached out a hand . . .

stopped an instant
right
in its tracks

turned it over
turned it round . . .

peered closely

saw strength

she saw love
she saw sadness

joy and tears

she saw the future now
she saw
the *now*
just past

an instant
of all she was

she *was*
she *might be*

gone

released

an instant

finding myself backwards

who was I
in the millennium year
twenty
zero zero?

who was I
in *seventy-two*
when politics changed
and the lefties
rose up?

who was I . . .

what was I *doing*
when apollo
went to the moon?

who was I
in nineteen fifty-six
when the olympics came
to melbourne?

who was *I*
back then?

I was forty-four
I was thereabouts
I was alone
and a loner

I was a teenage kid
still excited by
what might be
in my lifetime

my classmates and me
on the floor
in our assembly room

watching black and white
and grey
on the brand new
school *tee-vee*

I was just
a babe in arms
in germany
on the way from nowhere
to somewhere

who knew where?

who knew what?

who knew
anything
back then?

consequent

everything to come
starts from
this
moment

like a breath taken in
by the cosmos
to be released
as the flowing
of things

everything to come
began
from *then*

that moment

like a breath exhaled
by the cosmos
released to be

consequentially

nothing (at all)

my empty thought
is a void
of mind

an instant
drained
for the duration

bliss
oh bliss

a moment
of nothing
at all

a moment –
just one moment –
of emptiness
endured

and –
in the next –
I can think
again
with joy
of nothing

the novel one

she thought
a thought
that had no history

the novelty
made her warm
inside

she let it go –
she had to –
with no follow up

no *after*
thought

no residue

she only knew
that she had thought it
when she stumbled
over a –
now-empty –
space

she only knew
when it had
already gone

she would have liked
to know it
more intimately
to really *get*
what it was about

but the wind
whistled by
where it had been

and left her wondering

*what was my
novel thought?*

*what did it endure
before it reached me?*

*how long was it here
while I ignored it?*

*if it comes by again
how will I know?*

how will it change?

*when
will it come back to me?*

*will it ever
return?*

an event

I look at you
each glancing glance
the beginning

the start
of my attention
drawn your way

I look away

that glancing glance
is over

beginning looks
ending looks
instant looks
away

my event
with you
completed

see nothing

there is nothing
so full
of nothing
as emptiness

see it roll on –
vacant –
like a field of white
or less

or even *less*
than that

nothing
waiting to be filled

as time rolls by
empty grows
to fill all the world
that you can see

and for an instant
every part is gone
breadth and depth
and height

sensation

there is nothing
so full of nothing
as the blink
of an eye
that cannot see

your moment waits

the moment waits

a point
within a void

open
for a thought to happen by
and fill it

empty

biding in a null-field
action taking place
somewhere else
some-*when* else
away in the distance

>   *oh*
>   *for a little attention*
>
>   *oh*
>   *for a little*
>   *filling up with some thing*
>   *now*
>
>   *oh oh oh*
>   *a void*
>   *devoid*
>   *of any action*

how long
can a moment endure
this

>   *nothing*
>   *going on around here*

the moment ripe and ready
latent
potential at your call

come on by
with your intention

it is waiting
at your call

nothing (happening now)

things happen
from time to time

they happen here
and there

nothing
goes on forever
keeping every thing
apart

eternity
is the time that is lost
waiting
for something
to happen

and it starts again
right *now*

right

now

an hour of something

an hour lasts
for sixty minutes

each minute lasts
for seconds
in a sequence

measures
filled up
with time

but
an empty moment
lasts for a lifetime

stretching

forever

waiting for its time –
the right time –
to fill it
into a second

into a minute

for an hour
of some
thing

tick tock

how long was
nothing
if it was fuelled
by *nothing*?

I don't know

in the time
of *no time*
how long
was the time spent
waiting
for emptiness
to fill with something?

which part
of *everything*
contains something
now
right now?

will everywhere else
take forever?

when
will that happen . . .
(I don't know)

I
don't know

specimen of time

look at him now
poor specimen

would you believe
(no
how could you)
that he was born
so wealthy?

a babe in arms . . .

he had
everything

moment by moment
frittered away

look at him now
right here
before you . . .

a shell

just a shell
of what he was

so little remaining

look at him
right now

has he even understood
what he has spent?

what he has left?

he was born
pockets filled
with the coin

The Kiss Reverberant

with the coin
of time

now —
an old man —
all that remains
are moments

these very
few
last moments

running fast

so little time

running faster

what will be left
in another year?

look at me
now

the white space

if only I could write
this . . .

nothing

this . . .

blank space this
white
would go

would only remain
just ahead
of my encroaching pen

behind it

above

look back do you see?

writing
I banish the page
filled
as it is
with emptiness
and eternity

words words words

words words words

if only . . .

I would banish
nothing

two things (synchronicity)

two things
always happen
together

they are linked
forever

always

> *two things*
> *always happen*
> *at the same time*
>
> *they happen to happen*
> *the same time*
>
> *always*

does one thing
only happen
if the second thing
makes it so?

is it
the second
creating
the first?

> *does one thing*
> *make*
> *the second thing*
> *happen?*
>
> *is it one thing*
> *that always*
> *comes first?*

one thing
holding hands
with a second thing

maybe it is love
I just don't know

but those two things . . .

I always see them
together

they look so well
as two things

maybe that
is all I need
to know

a wall against

she wheeled
a barrow-load
of instants

mixed
a continuum
of moments she had melted
with a *zepto* or two
on a *planck*

laying this mortar
as foundation
she placed instant one . . .

instant two . . .

and so on

building a wall
against time

counting

hey
look at me

I'm counting
moments

one by one
so many pass
I can hardly
keep the score

I know a moment
is like
a nothing

and you and I
have so many –
birth
to grave

but
if I don't count them
do they have
meaning?

unnumbered
do they count
at all?

time
is a one-way street

moment markers
scattered
along the way

I
travel through my life
so swiftly . . .

The Kiss Reverberant

one moment
it is all there

and then . . .

I
am tallying my moments
because
you see
I'm no longer sure

unnumbered
they may not count
at all

on a continuum

any time
I do what I do
every time
is the same

it doesn't matter
when
if it is
that

and every time
I do it . . .

any time
I try . . .

the same
is the same
no matter now
or then

synchronicitous

two things
happen at the *same* time

two things happen
every time

every time
two things happen

every time
two things happen
at the same time

no coincidence
is this
synchronicitous bliss

what was, is

with every moment
something new

> *every instant*
> *builds*
> *on the last*

what was to be
is something
more than that

> *on and on*
> *extended*

every way
has another way

> *so break it down*
> *and break it*
> *down*

and so we go
multiplying
times tables

> *divide it*
> *to be smaller*

who knows
where or what
or when
the next way
will go?

The Kiss Reverberant

still it marches
on
and on

there is no way
of stopping time

multiply/divide

with every moment
something new

> *each instant*
> *builds*
> *on the last*

what was to be
becomes something
more than that

> *on and on*
> *extended*

every way
has another
way

> *so*
> *break it down*
> *and break it*
> *down*

and so we go
multiplying
time's tables

> *divide it*
> *to be smaller*

> *still*
> *the next*
> *is an instant*
> *further along*

The Kiss Reverberant

who knows
where or what
or when
the next way
will go?

> *there is no way*
> *to stop*
>
> *it must go on*

maybe me (in another moment)

where
did my lost moments
go?

I had in mind
to use them
when I found the time
like
just now

what could I
have done with them?

what *did* I do?

are they lost
only because
I can't recall . . .?

are they waiting
patiently
in some-when
to be recalled . . .

to be rejoiced?

those moments
just off to the side
of the road I took

moments
that might have been
other places
other times

another
maybe
me

worrying times

it only matters
if I think about it

only matters
if I feel

I think about
my feelings
from high
to
low

I feel
I think myself
into a state
sometimes

I think about that

I worry
some times

I worry

my illusion, I believe

my illusion
does not deceive

it is always
a lie

I can rely
on that
for
it is true

my illusion
is not *real*

it is only what I *choose*
to believe

and I know
that –
while *I* stay true –
my illusion will not

no no
my illusion
will not deceive

music of the duration

the duration
of a note
is really the duration
of a half a note
repeated

. . . is really the duration
of a quarter note
repeated

. . . is really . . .

breve

just breve

semi breve
semi breve again

each note will pass
in time

to be (for just a moment)

nothing cares
about who you are

breathing
doesn't know
that you're alive

the heart
is preoccupied

it is only pumping blood

it doesn't *feel*
a single thing
about you

only
the pulsing

paradise was lost
you know
while you were sleeping

wake up
wake up
this is the hour

wake up
wake up
this is your hour

wake
every instant
for just one hour

wake every instant
to be

aware of

I am aware

I am aware

I believe
that I know
this moment

I am not certain
of what went before

I am unsure
what
is to come

but
I believe
I am awake
right now

I believe
I am aware
and
I believe
it is *this*
moment

now now

now
is all there is

thinking
won't take me
back

feeling
won't carry me
forward

but *now*
is when I am . . .

who
and why

now is what I will do

now
now

now

I do not walk
a line
from *then*

I have not
set my cap
towards
another then
still to come

I am only what
I propose to be
right

now

right now

reading now

the future
is a dead space
as is
the past

I know this
now

I write this
now

you will read this
now

now I am writing

now
you are reading

my words are
immediate

no matter when

if you first read them
yesterday
you first read them
now

if you read them
tomorrow
when you will read them

is *now*

when am I

this
now
is consciousness

I am aware
of this moment
this moment

this moment
and no other

in *this* moment
I can be

and in no other

not *was*

not
still to come

it is only
only now
that I know

only in this instant
am
I

old note:new chord

there's a relative decline
in the drawn-out sound
of an old note

gently leaving itself
behind

sometimes
at some time
I
can hardly hear it
fade

and it's not playing
now
but the last strains
are a sweet song
that was so
present
then

there's a relative decline

a relative passing
of the presence
of that moment

the orchestra strikes
a new chord

the orchestra
strikes
the *new* chord

the orchestra is always
in the middle of the striking
of a new chord

that old note
is gone

surely swirly

he listened
to the future

heard it play
from an opening bar

> *whisky on the rocks please*

he knew the sound
knew the pitch
the tone

the note
sharp

in the moment
that surely shirley swirly hurly
certainly
must follow

and he listened

> *bee-bop-baaaa-aa*

to the madness
come
from three notes

> *ba-baaa-aa*

in succession

each one
extending in
its own
direction

The Kiss Reverberant

>　　*ba ba ba-baaaaa-baaaaa*

he
doomed to follow

into symphony
and a chaos

>　　*b-aaaaa*

>　　*dis-chord*

>　　*dis-chord baby*

he had not foreseen

with hands

>　　*boo-da-by-yyy*

tight
upon his ears
he sat

>　　*be-be-ba-buyy*

bent over

>　　*ba-ba*

in the corner

>　　*ba-*
>　　*baaaa-aaaa*

in the corner

at present

I was born
in the present time

I have lived there
all my life

this
is the place
I will die

> *now now now*

don't fret for me
I will live
forever

I *have* lived
forever

through all my years
in the present
time

forever

she knew the way
that the stone would fall

> *how far*
> *how high*
> *the trajectory*

from the moment
she fore-saw it

she knew the sound
the note would make

> *the tone*
> *the volume*
> *the feeling of*
> *vibration*

from the first brush
of her finger
against the string
when she fore-heard it

and in an instant
she made the future
stretch itself out
before her

a time of vision
and of sound
held
before they happened

a moment she could enter
forever

for just
a second

the loss

he lost his love
a long time ago

he lost his love
right now

it's a funny thing
about time

it's a funny thing
about love

the moment
it happened
he feels
happening again

and happening
again again
with each new
iteration

the architecture
of his heart
has never been rearranged
but waits
ready
for the return

the architecture
of his time
is a constant re-encounter

and all that
was
still
is

same again

does the future
come for me
no matter
what I do?

am I the only one
who steps
towards it?

will something happen
if I wait
only wait?

is doing nothing
still a something
that stirs a somewhere
in potential time?

I
am going nowhere

I am doing
nothing

tomorrow –
if tomorrow comes –
I plan
to do the same
again

I plan to do
just the same
again

learned time

I learned about yesterday
when I had to do
what I had already
done
but I had to do it
better

I remembered
I revised
I modified
yesterday
this morning

when did I learn
tomorrow?

how did I know
to make it seem
real
as real
as an aspiration
to being?

when did I begin
to let it matter
today?

beyond a shape, the senses

the past
did not happen today

when I woke up
it had gone

I don't know
what happened to it

but all that's left
is a yesterday *shape*

a yesterday *hole*

and today
keeps filling up
my senses

right now

yesterday gone

tomorrow un-begun

I am playing
right now
the whole orchestra

and I hear echoes
resound
across all time

I can still catch the tones
of yesterday
searching hard
to find a form

and
I feel the touch . . .

a questing kiss
searching for a timing
of its own

tomorrow
can hardly wait
to play
right now

enduring

I cannot make you
do anything

I do not try

all I do
is last
and
last

time
proves itself
my friend

I last
and I last
to see resistance come . . .

resistance go

until
you have ebbed

and done

while I –
still strong –
last
another while

habit

my habits
are a celebration
of a thing I did
once before

and a thing I did
once before

I don't remember
but I know

I celebrate my
some-when else
by doing a thing
again
that I know
now

just like

the past
persists
though only the moment
exists

it really should be
dead
by now

I think I keep it
out of habit
then pretend
somehow
that it's still real

I recall
a dance I did
once upon
a turn

like *this* . . .

I recall the dance
I did
something like
just now

something like
not long ago

I can *almost* twirl
that way again

I can almost
relive it
as though it was
as real
as *this*

I am in the habit
of persisting
with the realisation
of my memories

almost
they were just like
that

etching a return

she chipped into the rock

    I was here

etched it
deep
for duration

hoped that
one day
she could return
right here
right now

hoped
one day
she could remember

she glanced
at the ground
beside her feet

    I was here

penned
by a sandshoe
in loose scoria

on a tree
by penknife

on her arm
in scratches

her other arm
in ink

she hoped
one day
she would recall

hoped –
one day –
she might return

being and becoming

and if it already
is
what it
is not yet . . .

well
what of that?

don't we all know
it is only
what it will be
in time?

it is the thing

the thing that
it *really* is

and holds
all the power
needed

to become
just
what it is

seed

it is not
what it will be

it is everything
that may come

the possibilities are waiting
for inscription

it is
all that it might be
at *this*
this very moment

a magnet
for *if-maybe*

but
nothing
until then

to achieve the silence (of a violin)

the bow
attacks the string
to make it cry out
aloud

the bow attacks
the strings
and they all
cry

call it music . . .

call it
excitation . . .

call it the *melody*
of pain

call it –
if you will –
a form of violence

leave the bow
in its case
there will be
no assault
upon the string

leave the bow
inside its case
you will have
your silence

thirst the disintegration

the flour –
thirsty –
drinks
the water in

water –
in its way –
binds
to what has drunk it

water more
water more

water –
hungry –
eats
the flour

the flour
cannot separate
but
drifts apart
into a coloured wash

flour more
flour more
flour
so *much* more

thirst
builds again

thirst for water
more

learning to walk (creating a follower)

the shaping done
the baking done
she breathed a kiss
to bring him
into life

when his eyes opened –
fixed on her –
she could see
innocence . . .

readiness to learn

faith

absolute believing

then –
time and again –
she walked
placing her footsteps
into
her footsteps

he
did the same

and the habit formed
to walk that way

footstep
into footstep

he followed

wait . . . 'then' . . .

believe me
now
is but a taste
of *then*

what is to come
will be
much greater

now
you know

almost
it is the *only* thing
you know

but just you wait
just you wait

just you wait
and keep on
believing

instant belief

a little time

a little moment

just
an instant

was born

naked
knowing nothing
but
it had faith

a kind of faith

> *something*
> *would happen*

it had faith that
everything
would happen

some novelty

a meaning
even for small matter

a little time –
just a moment . . .

one small instant –
was born
believing
in an instant
just gone

soon to come

and so it endured

tattoo life

simultaneous spontaneity

discontinuous
continuity

the heart of being
in a throb
from temporal drums

syncopation
in the rhythm

the off-beat
of life

the feeling
that follows silence
the feeling
that makes a being
alive

tattoo you

tattoo you
alive

newborn breeze

when I am born
again
everything
is possible

nothing in my world
has failed

I set my sails

I wait the wind

when I am born
again
it is not certain
what
will be

if the wind
is in my quarter
I may sail away

I wait the wind

when I am born
again
it *may* be
nothing happens

it *may* be
I am doomed to wait
for a ruffling breeze
to pass

I wait
the wandering pleasure
of the wind

enscribed

a circle
rounds the triangle

a touch
a kiss
a gentling
of two

a two
that is
the one

the circle of the world

a being
in the heart

a touch
that could be
anything
a kiss that could be
everything

a gentling
for you
and for me

you
are my trinity

I
am your embrace

habitually me

I am in the habit
of repeating a habit

I do it often
to create a beat
for the rhythm of my living . . .

the rhythm of my *being* . . .

re-beat them often
that
is my habit

I have a habit
that beats *me me me me*

I am in the habit
of
repeating
myself

juiced up (as I recall)

my memory
is new and clear

I remember it
as I want it

almost
exactly
the way it was

but . . .

accuracy
gets boring
so I
embellish
a little

I embellish
at the edges

I know it is only a memory
but still
I have to *want*
to remember

so
I spice it up
a little bit

I give it juice
to keep it lively

my memory –
so new and clear –
is the way
I recall things
to be

memory of being

being
is a habit I have

I don't know
what else

don't know *how* else
to be

I am memories
laid down
one-on-one
incessantly

I would not want
to forget myself
so my habit
is remembering

remembering

all the things I *was*
I *am*

I remember
everything

I remember
all the time

remembering
I *am*

accidentally me

an accidental number
of accidental incidents
accidentally resulted –
instant
after instant –
in the gradual development
of a habit of repetition
that turned over time
that turned out
over long time
to –
kind of accidentally –
become the rhythm
that is
me

predictable change

this time
when I repeat myself
I'm going to do it
new

this time
I'll be tweaking
my old habits

I spend my life
repeating
because
how else will I know
what
I should do

this time
when I repeat myself
it's not going to be
the same

maybe
a *shimmy*
when I walk . . .

a *hiccup*
when I'm talking
to you . . .

put my hat on
back to front . . .

kiss with my eyes
open
not shut . . .

I'll change the cup-size
of my coffee
this time

yes
this time
I will repeat myself
brand new

I don't ever
want to be –
I'll repeat –
I do *not*
want to be
too
predictable

the habit of remembering

I want to be
the same
so you know me

I want to be different
so you want to

I want to *be*

and I will repeat
myself
I will *almost*
repeat myself
I will almost
be
just as I really was

I want you
to know me
the *same* way
that you knew me

hand
inside a glove

almost
the way it was
before

none like now

an instant
to actualize

a moment
to *be*
there is no
time
like the present

there is no
being
but now

accidentally here

you are nothing
but the sum
of accidents

from the first moment
of your life

nothing but an accident
upon an accident
upon
an accident

and here
now
you *are*

by chance
I
am here
too

fleet

here a moment
gone forever

gone
for good

now
is the fleeting thing

you may
want to read this
again

a habit of being (here)

I will be
here
at *this* time
every day

that
has become
my habit

accidentally

you
are nothing but a sum
of accidents
that happened
when you
didn't notice

I
am a series
of accidents . . .

I happened
in a moment
when I looked away

and I try to be
my self

sometimes
I resemble me
quite well

and you
try hard
to *be* your self
but
who
can remember
what *she* was

who can remember
except
by accident

together for a moment

hold myself
together
for a moment

hold myself
together for
another moment

for a moment
or two
this moment or two
I am
together

me (approximately)

I do things
by habit

I do not pay
too much
attention

I go through life
approximately

I approximate
me

if I
could only
focus

if I could
only *sharpen*
up

who knows
what I could . . .

approximately

near enough

as close to
me
as I
can be

a trace of me

I am tracing
today
over the top
of *yesterday*

they look to me
almost
as though
they are the same

the shape is there

the size is there

and –
if I look
very closely –

I can see me
a resemblance
of me
as I am
in the tracing
of today

in yesterday

better

I am a copy
of myself

    of myself

      of myself

          of myself

always
reborn

only . . .

better

aware the moment

I was aware
of *that*

and
I was aware
of *that*

and
I was aware . . .

how do I know
my consciousness . . .

that
I am alive . . .

if not by
awareness
of the things
that are
in my moments?

each I know

I give my
life
to each moment
that I know

each moment
I know
I am
alive

this
is the time
of my life

as change

every moment
I am changing

every moment
changes
me

and I –
returning compliments
and favours –
change time
to reflect
me
as *I*
change

woven

I weave
my fabric

       instant one . . .

       instant two . . .

I weave
the fabric
of my time

and
I endure

duration, habit and progress

I group my
instants
in their
one-by-ones

place them
close enough
to make
duration

so –
my instants –
they go on
and on
the way I do

I exist
inside my habits
where I train myself
in *who*
to be

this education
is the *be*-ing
and again –
as before –
I will
endure

and progress
along my
instant-line

habit
after habit
until . . .

I get a shock
sometimes
but
I arrive . . .

again . . .

at *me*

you I know

in loving *you*
I know
myself

I know the needs
I own

I know
the ways
to appease them

I know
the deficiencies
this creature
carries

I know who
I am
in
the contemplation
of love
for you

is mystery

the universe
beautiful

is
the universe
meaningful

and the face
is the home
of mystery

mine now

with the peaking
of my
maturity

I can no longer
lay the burden
of custody
for my dreams

my *fondest* dreams

at the feet
of tomorrow

The Dialectic of Duration

pushing for change

it was
a *physical*
thing . . .

his argument
with time

periodically
he found himself
in disagreement

> *with the pace*
>
> *with the effects*
>
> *the things allowed*
>
> *the things*
> *not*
>
> *the changes*
> *that led from*
> *intimate familiarity*
> *to*
> *strangeness*
>
> *alienation*

alright
call it
a *fight*

at one level
he *knew*
he could not win

time
is
an *inexorable*

but . . .

still . . .

he pushed it
back

back

like a dam wall
retreating up the river valley
and herding water
upstream
towards the spring

towards
the younger water
that was
its source

he pushed . . .

retreated . . .

retrieved . . .

then
he relaxed

and allowed it
to flow
forward
once again

this time
hoping

working

to make it happen
differently

to make it happen
right

one moment - an intuition (of autumn)

my heart
knew
the summer flowed –
an ebb –

away

but
in my mind –
when I looked back –
each day
stood
as one

alone

> *the day*
> *that it shone*
>
> *the day that it rained*
>
> *the day*
> *I slept until*
> *my lunch*
> *had passed*
>
> *the day that came*
>
> *the day*
> *just gone*

each stood alone
as summer
flowed over me

and now –
today –
a leaf will turn

from green
to all the shades
of brown

and –
on a day
to come –
each leaf
will choose its time
to fall away

one
by one

they
will go

wishing (the end) away

she knew
an end
would come

an end
to morning
though
she had just woken

an end to night
as –
even now –
the first signs
of light
crept toward her
from the eastern horizon

an end
to the daily grind
that saw her rise
before the sun today
to attend
her workplace

an end
to the simplicity
of fruit-bread toast
on more idle days

an end
to her ability to think

to follow a thought
from one
point
through a line
of logic
to a conclusion
in a poem

an end
to next breaths

to life

she knew
it would come
and wished –
fervently –
that it would
not

wandering

he found that his thought
had
broken free

afloat
upon its own
desires

separated

almost out . . .
. . . of touch

not needing
him
to be
complete

he watched it
leave

saw it grow
smaller
into the distance

toward the western sun

sinking
with the orb

he . . .

left alone
bereft

wondering

if . . .

when
morning comes

will that wandering thought . . .

my
wandering thought

come back home
to
me

instant nothing

it was an instant
of time

when *nothing*
happened

I know
because I
was watching

I
looked at it

up
and down

I considered it . . .

nothing

it took me an instant –
no more –
but I wrote it down

everything
that occurred

as follows:

.
.
.

years ago

the stuff
of time

the *stuff*
of
space

how do you fill
to the brim
an *idea*

fill *time*
with doing

fill space
with things that
are

then wait
the long while
with *time*
on your hands . . .

make yourself
the room you need
to move . . .

it will pass
too fast

and
it will always
be too small

until
the less you need
becomes the more
that you want

The Kiss Reverberant

what you hoped for
once

fades
to be years
ago

the problem (with his hat)

he said

> I am worried
> about
> my hat
>
> I know
> it is nothing
> special
>
> just
> a felted hat
> with a braided band
>
> it has a narrow
> brim
> that suits me
>
> that suits my head
> if you like
>
> but now —
> when I think
> of it —
> I worry
>
> .
> .
> .
>
> I know

he said

> that my hat is —
> strictly speaking —
> quite lifeless

The Kiss Reverberant

and I know too
that where I place it
it
must stay

I see that —
on the hook
right there —
it hangs obediently
just as I believe
that it should

yet
when I turn
away . . .

I find
I can no longer be sure
that it is
still there

waiting

un-stoppered: the rightness

I have it

he said

*here
in the bottle*

he brandished
a brown flask
stoppered
and sealed

*it has taken me
all these years
but
I have it
here
at last*

*in my bottle
is the memory
of a time
that slipped by me*

*a time when
I could have done . . .*

could have been
so much

all I need to do . . .

he was chuckling
to himself
perhaps *too*
gleefully

The Kiss Reverberant

> *all I need*
> *to do*
> *is un-stopper it*

I may have looked
a little
skeptical

for he almost shouted
at me

> *don't you see*
> *I will be engulfed*
> *by the time*
> *that I so wish*
> *to live over*

I can change

I can remedy

I can put
oh
so much
right

> *all I need to do*
> *is*
> *to open . . .*

temporary permanent destruction

she was aware
that
every time
she closed her eyes . . .

each occasion
of sleep
saw the temporary –
permanent –
destruction
of every thought
and every idea
that comprised the world

her world only
it is true
but
from her personal position
her world
was everything

all that *was*
all that *is*

most of the time
this destruction
was an abstract thing

an idea
to mull over
sometimes
with her eyes closed

as a test

gradually though
she found herself
sleeping
less

The Kiss Reverberant

staring
painfully
for long periods of time

imagining
what would happen
to the world . . .

to *her* world . . .

if a day came
when she could not
open
her eyes

knowing
that day
was coming

endurance found

he wondered
where the time
had gone

for
in truth
he was old now
though
inside himself
he was no older

no older
than he had ever been

casting through his mind

memories

memories

yes
there was an equation
to be found there

he had
endured
through all
that he had experienced

the time he had spent
was all there –
locked up
within his recollections –

and as he drifted
in among the events
that comprised him –
all the past
that he had lived –

The Kiss Reverberant

he became aware
of the experience
that was still to come

the *end* of his
endurance

his *times*

he found
all the time he had spent –

> *the good time*
> *and the bad*
>
> *the empty time*
> *and the fulfilled*
>
> *the troubled*
> *and the carefree*

and he found
his death
calmly
waiting the end

more is less

I fill my time
as full
as I can

I cram it . . .

something like
a suitcase

the fuller I fill it
and the more
I can squeeze
into every possible
instant
the shorter
my time
seems to grow

was (gone)

with every change
I die
a little

mourn
with me
the one that
I was

who I am
remains to be seen

but
with *this* change
who I *was*
has gone

Bachelard Source Materials

Gaston Bachelard, French Philosopher lived from 27 June 1884 to 16 October 1962. The series of poems and poetry in this book has drawn inspiration from the following publications by Bachelard, translated into English.

Intuition of the Instant by Gaston Bachelard (1932) Eileen Rizo-Patron (Translator) Northwestern University Press, 2013

The New Scientific Spirit, by Gaston Bachelard (1934), A. Goldhammer (Translator) Beacon Pr; 1st Edition (1984)

The Psychoanalysis of Fire, by Gaston Bachelard (1938), A.C. Ross (Translator) (1964).

Lautréamont, Gaston Bachelard (1939), Robert S. Dupree (Author), James Hillman (Author), Dallas Institute Publications; Reprint Edition (2012)

Water and Dreams: An Essay on the Imagination of Matter by Gaston Bachelard (1942), Edith R. Farrell (Translator) (1983.

Air and Dreams: An Essay on the Imagination of Movement, by Gaston Bachelard (1943), Edith R. Farrell (Translator), Frederick Farrell (Translator) Dallas Institute Publication Dallas Institute Publications (1988)

Earth and Reveries of Will: An Essay on the Imagination of Matter by Gaston Bachelard (1943), Kenneth Haltman (Translator) Dallas Institute Publications (2002)

Earth and Reveries of Repose: An Essay on Images of Interiority by Gaston Bachelard (1948), Mary McAllester Jones (Translation), Dallas Institute Publications (2011)

Dialectic of Duration. Gaston Bachelard (1950), Mary McAllester Jones (Translator), Rowman & Littlefield Publishers; (2016)

The Poetics of Space by Gaston Bachelard (1958), Maria Jolas (Translator) Penguin Classics (1964).

The Poetics of Reverie, by Gaston Bachelard (1960), Daniel Russell (Translator) Beacon Press; New Ed Edition (1971)

The Flame of a Candle, by Gaston Bachelard, (1961), Joni Caldwell (Translator) Dallas Institute Publications (1988).

The Right to Dream by Gaston Bachelard (1970), J.A. Underwood

(Translator) Dallas Institute Publications (1988)
Fragments of a Poetics of Fire, by Gaston Bachelard, Kenneth Haltman *(Translator), Dallas Institute Publications (1988)*
On Poetic Imagination and Reverie, by Gaston Bachelard, Colette Gaudin *(Translator) Spring Publications; (2014)*

Author Information

Frank Prem has been a storytelling poet for more than forty years and spent his working life in various parts of the public psychiatry system in Victoria, Australia.

His work has been published in magazines, e-zines, and anthologies both in Australia and internationally, and he has performed and recorded his poetry as spoken word. He has published more than 35 poetry and picture-book collections.

Frank is an Adjunct Research Associate with the School of Education at Charles Sturt University, Australia.

He and his wife live in the beautiful township of Beechworth, in North East Victoria.

Connect with Frank

Find Frank at his website www.FrankPrem.com, or through Social Media online at Facebook, X (Twitter), Instagram and YouTube.

Other Published Works

A Poetry Archive
A Poetry Archive – Volume 1 (2024)
A Poetry Archive – Volume 2 (2024)
A Poetry Archive – Volume 3 (2024)
A Poetry Archive – Volume 4 (2024)
A Poetry Archive – Volume 5 (2025)
A Poetry Archive – Volume 6 (2025)

Memoir
Small Town Kid (2018)
The New Asylum (2019)

Picture Poetry Series
A Lake Sambell Walk (2021)
A Few Places Near Home (2023)
Pilgrim Volume 1 - Illustrated by Leanne Murphy (2024)

Children's Picture Books
The Beechworth Bakery Bears (2021)
Waiting for Frank-Bear (2021)
On Allium Avenue (2025)

Bachelard Interpreted
A Choir of Whispers (2024).
A Cleansing Flame (2024)
Real Weight (2025)
A Flight Of Ideas (2025)
An Ocean of Purity (2025)
The Kiss Reverberant (2025)

Speculative Poetry
The Garden Black (2022)
A Specialist At The Recycled Heart (2022)
The Cielonaut (2024)

A Love Poetry Trilogy
Walk Away Silver Heart (2020)
A Kiss for the Worthy (2020)
Rescue and Redemption (2020)
Alive Is What You Feel (2023)

Natural Disasters
Devil In The Wind (2019)
Of Drought and Fire (2025)
SMALL Change (2025)

War and Conflict
Sheep On The Somme (2021)
From Volyn To Kherson (2023)

Free Verse
Herja, Devastation With Cage Dunn (2019)
Pebbles to Poems (2020)
Ida: Searching for The Jazz Baby (2023)
White Whale (2024)

What Readers Say

<u>*Small Town Kid*</u>

A modern-day minstrel. Highly recommended.
—A. F. (Australia)

Small Town Kid is a wonderful collection.
—S. T. (Australia)

<u>*Devil In The Wind*</u>

Trust me, this book will stay with you. Bravo!
—K. K. (USA)

Moving, beautiful, and terrible. I was left with a profound sense of respect, as well as a reminder that we should never take for granted every precious every moment of life.
—J. S. (South Africa)

<u>*The New Asylum*</u>

Words can't do justice to the emotional journey I travelled in (reading this collection).
—C. D. (Australia)

If I had to pick one book over the past year that has truly resonated with me, this would be it.
—K. B. (USA)

<u>*Walk Away Silver Heart*</u>

Instantly grips you by the throat in his step-by-step story of survival. Bravo!
—K. K. (USA)

Outstanding!
—B. T. (Australia)

A Kiss For The Worthy

A Celebration of Life Written in Thoughtful Bursts of Poetic Expression
—C M C (United States)

With every verse, I found myself reflecting about myself, my life, and the world.
—K

Rescue and Redemption

The passion of love in its many forms explored by one for another.
—J L (United States)

I've enjoyed every word, every breath. Every moment within the life of these stories.
—C D (Australia)

Sheep On The Somme

Museums and archivists take note–sell this in your gift shops, preserve it in your archives. Professors, teachers–share with your students.
—A R C (United States)

(This) book is a beautiful and graphic tribute to all those brave men and women who gave their lives for their countries between 1914 and 1918.
—R C (South Africa)

Ida: Searching for The Jazz Baby

I found myself deeply moved by the presentation of Ida's elusive, illusionary life.
—E G (United States)

He gives her a depth and vulnerability that the press didn't.
— A C (United Kingdom

The Garden Black

Prem creates verse that illuminates our world, its experiences and history.

—S C (United Kingdom)

Prem's poetry reminds that life is fragile and fleeting ... both harsh and beautiful.

—D G K (Canada)

A Few Places Near Home

The author has captured many beautiful images in this book, and is a wonderful photographer as well as a poet. This book would make a beautiful coffee table book filled with moving prose to make us ponder with gorgeous accompanying images.

—D K (Canada)

www.FrankPrem.com

www.ingramcontent.com/pod-product-compliance
Lightning Source LLC
Chambersburg PA
CBHW052039070526
44584CB00020B/3165